Published I
Imagine

©Copyright 2005
Helen L Barker & Andrew C Brown

The right of Helen L Barker & Andrew C Brown
to be identified as the authors of the work has been asserted by them in
accordance with the Copyright, Designs and Patents Act 1988.

All Rights Reserved
No reproduction, copy or transmission of this publication
may be made without written permission.
No paragraph of this publication may be reproduced,
copied or transmitted save with the written permission or in accordance
with the provisions of the Copyright Act 1956 (as amended).
Any person who does any unauthorised act in relation to
this publication may be liable to criminal
prosecution and civil claims for damage.

First published in 2005

ISBN: 0-9550576

Printed by:
Imagine
1 Carr Street
Liversedge
West Yorkshire
WF15 6EE

To the person who buy's this book.

I wish you well and hope your dreams are true

With Love Andrew :o)
 x

Thankyou for all your support.
 Best Wishes,
 Hela
 x.

FOREWORD

It was a great honour to be asked to be patron of Reuben and friends and I didn't hesitate to say yes and give everyone connected to the charity my full support. I hope it will be a long association that will benefit the hardworking team behind the organisation

Duncan Wood

"Q. How do you fit a six foot television presenter into a child's play hospital?".

A. With great difficulty!

Unless of course Dr Reuben is at home and ready for consultation, then you're in and hooked on his every word.
That was how I first met a remarkable little boy as I crawled around his living roomfloor into his make believe world of medicine.
Sadly Reuben relies on constant hospital treatment in the real world.
His many needs have inspired a group of dedicated friends to create the charity Reuben and Friends, to raise money and awareness of his rare condition.
This is their very first publication and knowing their commitment to the cause I'm sure it won't be the last

Gift Page

This book is a gift

To ....

From ....

Dedications

These poems are dedicated to Reuben and my sweet children Harry and Molly: through them I have the pleasure of seeing the gift of life every day.

Helen L Barker

These poems are dedicated to my lost beloved son Daniel, whose kindness was needed in a different world.
Also to my other children Sophie and Nathan, whom I love with all my heart. I miss them so much when I am not by their side.

And of course Reuben, a little boy who I have never had the privilege of meeting but from whose courage I find strength to face each day.
Our children show us the way. We just need to look from time to time.

Andrew C Brown

We hope all parents find some comfort from this book; we had so much pleasure and sadness writing it. The biggest lesson we learned is our greatest gift is our children. They will continue to inspire and give us hope, courage and true happiness every day. The only thing they ask for is our Love

Helen L. Barker and Andrew C. Brown, 19th February 2005

Explanatory note from Helen L. Barker and Andrew C. Brown

1st January 2005 Text Message:

"A very happy new year to nine of the most amazing, selfless, generous and talented ladies I know. We are so blessed to have such wonderful friends!"

It was 31st October 2003 when Michelle and Peter finally received confirmation that their three-year-old son Reuben had been diagnosed with a form of Pure Red Cell Aplasia. So rare there is no name attached to his precise symptoms, and no known cure. If no exact bone marrow match could be found then the only treatment would consist of regular blood transfusions to keep him alive.

I walked into the kitchen where Michelle, part of our NSPCC fund raising team, was cooking mushy peas to serve as part of our pie & pea supper at the Halloween Party we had organised. She told us about Reuben's illness. There was a look of total helplessness, bewilderment and fear at the circumstances that now faced her family.

Our group became known as Reuben & Friends. It is our hope that we will one day raise sufficient funds to initiate a research project into this and closely associated blood diseases. Our current fund-raising activities aim to educate our community about Pure Red Cell Aplasia and we help to promote awareness of the National Blood Service and Bone Marrow Registry.

I had never written a poem before until I met Andy who inspired me with his poetry; it was his suggestion that we combined our efforts and place our raw emotion on paper to reflect our innermost feelings.
This is my first attempt at writing, and my wish is that the following words and poems will bring inspiration and hope to all who read them and, like me, count on friends to see to a positive future. Something not quite right with the last phrase? Doesn't seem to follow, to me.

HLB

When Helen told me the story of this amazing little boy I was in South Korea complaining about the food and simple trivial things that are not really important. I had suffered the agony of losing a dear son, who had to leave this life because he was needed elsewhere. I began to remember the pain of that traumatic time. We as human beings should do all we can to support each other in difficult times. This book of poems expresses our true feelings and is written without fear of emotion.
I hope the poems we have written bring inspiration hope and rekindle found memories of precious times. Life is for living. Make each day a special memory.

ACB

Profiles

Helen Barker works in technical sales for a UK manufacturer of biocides. She lives in Cleckheaton with her two children, Harry and Molly. Helen was born in Mirfield, West Yorkshire in October 1966. She gained a BSc (Hons) Degree in Chemistry with Business Administration at Kingston Polytechnic in 1990. After several years working in London she moved back to Yorkshire to start a family.

She was first inspired to write when she met Andrew Brown in October 2004.

Andrew C Brown is a company director who has had the privilege to have worked and lived in most parts of the world.

Andrew was born in Liverpool in April 1962 and is from a humble background. He served ten years in the military before beginning a career in the Oil and Gas Industry. Andrew has three Children: Daniel (Deceased, his memory lives on in all our hearts) Sophie, and Nathan.

Acknowledgements

My thanks go to my parents for their love and support, to my children for their tireless optimism and to my friends for just being there.

Thank you to my fellow Reuben & Friends team members: Dawn, Gill, Helen H, Helen L, Karen, Kim, Michelle, Suzanne and of course Michelle GM for all their help.

To Andy, who has given me the confidence to pick up the pen and the inspiration and encouragement to put my thoughts in writing, thank you.

Helen x

My thanks go to my children, for giving me hope and showing me the real meaning of love and the purity of childhood innocence, where the priority in life is to enjoy each day and learn from the experience.

I am not the most reasonable person and I carry so many weaknesses, each day I try to address my failings and present a decent person to the world.

Finally I would like to thank Helen Barker: she offered me the opportunity to do something worthwhile and find something inside me that I thought I had lost. Her untiring effort and commitment had no boundaries.

Most of all I would like to thank a special person called Reuben, without knowing it Reuben inspired me to understand the meaning of life. He faces his challenge every day without complaint.

Andrew x

Contents

The Glass House 8	Part of You 59
A Safe Haven 9	Friendship 60
New Girl 10	Past on a Stage. 61
A True Friend 11	Tramp 62
Alright Now 12	Pink and Warm 63
In my well-being. Finding you 13	India 64
Talking to the Grey Man 14	Reach in Darkness 65
Corporate Entertainment 15	Red Wine Friends 66
Visit to Chesterfield 16	Remember 67
Island in the Ocean 17	You Wrote This 68
Diving 18	Remembering Love 69
Just Waiting 19	9-5 70
Look Beyond 20	Running Through Tunnels. 71
Eight 21	Friends 72
Jan 22	Searching 73
Isobel 23	His Devotion 74
A brief moment 24	Sit for a While 75
Fox 25	Doves 76
A Stand for a Fool 26	Surround 77
The Dark Room 27	The Metronome 78
A Time for glory 28	The Ashtray of Life 79
Twelve 29	The Oarsman 80
Always plan something 30	The Cottage by the Lake 81
Coracle 31	The Bag Lady 82
At Last 32	The Curtain Falls 83
Corridor 33	The Composer 84
Dad 34	The Market Place 85
Leaf 35	Puzzle 86
Dedicated to a Special Friend ... 36	The Old Man 87
Moon Walking 37	In the Sand 88
Dry Your Tears With Love 38	The Power of a Minute 89
Seagulls over Barnsley 39	Hugh 90
Embrace 40	The Short Journey 91
The Red Dress 41	The Day Ahead 92
Flat Pack Furniture 42	The Sweet Cherry Blossom 93
The flag 43	Without Friends 94
High Wire Annie 44	The WAR is Over 95
How to Write Poetry 45	Plate 96
The Coconut 46	Touch 97
I Forgot The Rain 47	My Watery Environ 98
The Alchemist 48	True Life with Love 99
If 49	Loch Dreams 100
Learning to Swim 50	Walking by your Side 101
Journey by Taking the First Step ... 51	The Palm Reader 102
Shopping Days 52	Walls 103
Look Through the Window 53	Daisy Chains 104
A kiss 54	We Came to Visit 105
Love at the Table 55	Angels 106
Octopus 56	Sense on Sense 107
Old and Forgotten 57	
Radio Frequency 58	

The Glass House

Instead of resting on the plateau I flutter looking forever upward
Confused by darkness, unable to accurately define the prism
There's no likelihood of clarifying intent until death.
Clothed in my cape of dazzling facts
I fly higher, driven by a blind optimism.
Fascination pushes me further towards the light
Perseverance has more effect than any frantic rage
and persistently I battle the wafts of breeze to reach my goal.
As the light impels me I feel the intensity of this heat and
in awe I stare mesmerised at my improbable angel
My cape dissolving in his gaze

I want him to take me in his sturdy hand
Selfishly he draws the essence, but only to press too tightly.
He propels me headlong into the sun and in one moment of spellbound
enlightenment, absolute purity is blighted by reality.
My heart is crystallised and splinters with false promises.
Foolish hopes rip my wings apart and gossamer crumbles to dust.
He smashes our little glass temple and the fragments fall painfully one by one, each piece an echo of a previous life
Inextricably (?) the shards of tears don't touch him he's cocooned by misogyny, distrust
and fear.
The flimsy specks float away insignificantly on the breezes I had once battled.
My ashes now scattered in his reckless wake.

Helen L. Barker

A Safe Haven

A comfortable moment in a troubled time, we come to look for true meaning. I am reaching out to find a place of sanctuary in a world of turmoil.
I feel the presence of my soul with no toil.

Darkness will take me through to light and when the warmth tingles my skin I will feel a comfortable surround. This moment will live in my soul and continue to grow through any twisted fate you prepare for me.

Do not linger too long. Come with me to the cottage of happiness, we can warm ourselves by the fire, drink tea and eat cucumber sandwiches. The moment will not fade and we will never grow old. Our end does not stand before us.
We have no havoc here!!

It has no shadow, and only the sun shines.

Andrew C Brown

New Girl

Cast aside with a new girl label
sewn diligently and deftly by the old gang
together enforcing this unfortunate stain forever

Fumbling to fix the unfix-able I want to give up
Anger forces the blunt needle painfully stabbing a flushed complexion
and frustration asks how could I not know?

Popularity prettiness good humour
Never to be within my grasp
but stupidly I persist in petty triviality for the sake of form

The warm feeling seeps further than the dread now
and reality smacks her face into my tear stained incompetence
I can no longer ignore her, so shamefully my secret is known

Helen L. Barker

A True Friend

When I am sad you make me laugh, when I smile you smile too.
When I need you I only ask and you appear with my protection.

I can never be lonely, I will never face the torment of life, you offer and I take. What can I give?
What gift can I deliver to you, how can I repay the reason for my happiness?

Never far away, always near, with each moment of my sadness you offer truth, my selfishness is swept aside and you shower me with the will and affect my state of mind, how can I repay you?

I sometimes wallow and cannot change, I look up and see your hands outstretched and I reach and hold strong. You ask for nothing in return. Each time I stumble you pick me up dust my back and push me gently in the way of happiness. It's like the sail of a ship leading its crew to land, safety and home. The true love of home. The oak door allows you to pass into a world of moments, the smile of childhood and the tenderness of my surround.

When I need you, you always forsake your time for me. I have nothing in return. What you see before you is my moment of weakness, I need to drown in your strength, I nestle to you heart my body steals the warmth from your arms.

I place my hand in yours, lead me from my turmoil and forgive me once again. Tomorrow I will feel the shame, but now I sleep.

How do I describe this, it's not so simple for me, but I can say it in one word. Friendship!!!
A true friend will give and never take.

Andrew C Brown

Alright Now

The broken glass beneath her feet no longer crackles
She feels no pain underfoot
Bruises and soreness must be numbed in red-rose wine
Taint of stale cigarettes and booze are no longer detectable
No feeble uttering feigning togetherness
Trembling she walks alone looking for the moonlight
She is ready to face her only love again
Reaching out for any tall dark and handsome
Her fingers pass through the flickering flames to a delight beyond
In a brief moment desire releases shame and contempt
Unaware of this release the search will begin again

Helen L Barker

In my well-being. Finding you.

How can we stand in the rain and watch as tyrants disturb our peace in moments of happiness? I am just a simple man with humble pride without stock of wealth, I ask nothing from you, but in my moment of fear you offer me anger, what can I do beyond this point?

To stand as a militant can only lead to devastation and pure destruction, why not help me, stand by my side and create the defiance that is needed to remove such disgust from our existence.

Stand with me I beg you, walk the lonely barricades with a strong heart and a sense of pride. We can strike out with conviction and honesty to remove the hatred that forms part of our very life.

Search my soul and you will find no answers. I am a man with only dreams of my peace. My soul can only hold a single drop of life; the burden is too great to carry a simple monument of humanity.

Do not judge me; stand with me so we can dilute this menace and return to our confirmed destination, do not pre-judge or even make an excuse for the unfortunate. If I can reach beyond the fear of this turmoil I can offer my strong allegiance to the truth.

I cast out all tyrants, be gone with a whimper and return no more. Your potent breath does not warrant my fear, the direction I walk you have no place at my side.

I have my well-being and I command myself respect. Leave my soul and walk alone, I search a path, I ask my friend to join me, help me in my quest, together we are stronger, we hold the passion to reach the blackness and create the philosophy to drive our direction forward in the style we asked for.

Andrew C Brown

Talking to the Grey Man

You can spend your whole life wading through treacle
Speaking in syrupy tones and looking for your own personal interpreter
You may never find her, the one to show you the precipice

But in my dreams I stand on the edge of the precipice and look down
The view is scary and exhilarating
Fascination (or stupidity) is enough and I dare to dive headlong

Surprisingly inexperience forges its own conduit through the viscous slush
and a rush of excitement takes my breath and gives it freedom
Now unstuck, everything is understood

Helen L Barker

Corporate Entertainment

Do you pound the pavement for a reason? Each click of a heel makes a distinctive sound. Is she just waiting for a simple act?

The cleanliness of touch has to be paramount; in this priority we call this a business. I have come to visit the paper house and isolate myself from the reality of corporate image. The suit and tie is of navy blue. The train journey has stopped at the final station and I am walking the platform to find another day.

In a sky of rooftops and TV aerials, I search for a colour of blue, in a slander of murky grey. A leather armchair holds the responsibility for the next final decision. A telephone conversation will hold the prospect of a healthy bonus in a Swiss bank.

Some shapes do not fit into the outline and we only force the object into a very uncomfortable position. Do we have the control or do we just pretend?

Andrew C Brown

Visit to Chesterfield

I veil my self-hatred in black and concentrate on my unworthy goal
Whirring and thumping sounds beat in my heart and grubs leer behind dirty muscles.
Ignoring them I move closer now stepping out of the fog

From bitter to just cold I survey the watery coffin but it's not the sight of the laying out
or even each beast bobbing absurdly up and down, but the stench. It hits you hard.

Swallow and plan your tactics
March slowly and purposefully along each gangway
Collect those heirlooms that weren't yours for the taking and make your way towards
their final resting place

An elegant pile of wealth, materialism, disgust and disbelief at the trade: our trade
but we persist, don't we?
Out of each death a wage for me and you

Helen L. Barker

Island in the Ocean

Imagine yourself on a desert Island, a small desert island, surrounded by a deep blue ocean. You are completely alone with no companion, friend or soul mate. Each day you search for a dream, a destiny to follow. But on a desert island you are isolated in self-awareness.
Each day you look inwards trying to find the true meaning of your existence and trying to understand your mind, learning the meaning of a peaceful harmony.

With romance comes a deeper happiness, however without romance happiness still survives. You will have to search in lonely dark places.
You open a door and find only sadness and despair. Don't close that door: leave it open, but don't go into the room. Stand in the doorway and observe the anguish.

If you pass through the doorway you may never come back.
Search your desert island; find the beauty in the ocean, the sand and the life that surrounds you. Watch the birds fly, watch the fish swim. See the real life all around. Look at yourself: don't analyse the dark side, only analyse the good.

Remember your true feelings, absorb your true purpose, look inward, and find your real soul.
The inner search maybe painful and emotional, but the feelings will be worth the small amount of suffering. At the right moment your life will fall into line and be complete. You will understand the simplicity of life.

When you have seen all, you may leave your desert island ready to accept life in all its glory, you will understand more and you will follow your dreams.

Andrew C Brown

Diving

He plunges in and cold sensations rapidly become warm, inviting
His destiny lies in the freedom of the deep
He is in search of the forbidden 'one'
The first: a perfect orb but this is not his quest
He dives deeper for a truer prize
Beneath rocks and barriers he thought impenetrable he finds her
His knife brands a delicate line along the rim
Despair at the repulsion and his abhorrent lust are pushed aside by the stronger
Love and trust and utter faith
He shows her preciousness, her wholeness, her nacreous beauty to the world
In her he finds his own completeness

Helen L. Barker

Just Waiting

How can I breathe when you leave, how can you feel the smooth touch of my hand on your body. When you look at me I can feel your eyes burning into my soul. Now I am blind. I am lost in a world of sorrow.
I hunger for your love, the love that will never un-die.
You have taken from me and left? Only a memory; you have destroyed what has no meaning or purpose. The taste of you, it haunts my dreams and the coldness of loneliness wraps me with a blanket of pain.
I cannot reach out to you when I need to cry, I cannot reach out to you when my fear controls my life.
You are the only one who can bring me to my knees, I fall in darkness with no feeling, I cannot crawl back from my bleeding heart.
I lie down in an ocean fall of tears, and I drown in sadness. I have emptied my heart and you take everything with you. All that remains is sorrow. Don't turn to take the emptiness. I remain with no meaning. I can no longer breathe, I search for the reasons but with no answers I cannot find the questions.
Tell me why did you hurt me so? Did I not feed your hunger for love? Did I not hold your hand, did I not reach out with my heart and offer the warmth of my arms.
I saw it in your eyes, please take my soul and return to me, in a dream. Let me taste you again. In a time and place I can remain.
I will wait for you. I may stand-alone for a time. I look back at the goodbye and see the love drift from all meaning.
How can I breathe? Now I stand alone, just waiting......

Andrew C Brown

Look Beyond

When I look I cannot see you, when I reach I cannot touch you. When I search I cannot find you. Each day I wake with the pain, each day I live through this nightmare again and again.
Where did you go? Why did you leave my side?
I search each part of my heart to find the happiness that was your life, the smile that took me to my existence, the touch of your love with moments of blissfulness and sweet memories.
The twisted thorns wrap my heart, the blood that drips so cold with no red. I have no reason to breathe; I have no reason to Cherish; I have no reason to live my life. The torment that binds me brings my soul to its knees; I fall in anger before your feet. I cannot beg, I only wallow in self-pity. I start ripping the flesh from my body, burning my eyes with evil and disgust.
I drowned in sorrow I feel the filth that wraps my dignity, I reach for you, I want to cradle you, do not scorn me, I have no reality, I wish you would press your lips on my brow and force this darkness to my light.
I want to remember your life with delight, take me beyond that door, take my burden from my back, allow me to stand, my knees bleed from the stone, and my back bleeds from the tormented flesh that peels from my poor existence. The blood of my life washes away into a river of dilution, I cannot save myself, I hear you and I see you, I want to stand by your side.

Take my hand, the time has come for me to join you.

Andrew C Brown

Eight

She beneath the surface, her hair flows around her
Her skin is soft and white and perfectly smooth
She gestures to come closer

Passers-by fleetingly stop and peer in and nod admiringly
But not at her, in a kind of narcissist way
But who cares she won't know

She reaches up towards their advancement and holds out cupped hands
She speaks in watery words trying to make them understand
They nod and smile and move on

She moves away from the surface now
She continues to exist and waits to live

Helen L. Barker

Jan

In a moment of horror I call for you, I reach out to hold your hand, if I feel the warmth of your fingertips I know tomorrow will come.

In my nightmares I search for you, the fear melts away in your dominating presence, how can I live without you?

I have only the time we shared together; if I need you will you come to my side. Your eyes are like the diamonds of my mind; they sparkle with the lust of my Arabian heart. Search for me as I search for you; find me in the turmoil of my battle.

In my fear you see my weakness, you hold my life with a delicate hand, and your sweet taste can only forge the strength between us. If I can see only love in your eyes, how can I not forgive this anger and pain?

In darkness and solitude you are my light, each spark of brightness brings new life and purpose, how can I ever repay you?

Andrew C Brown

Isobel

I have only one regret, that I didn't hold you in my arms and tell you how much we loved you and how much you mattered and how life wouldn't be the same without you. How you had to hold onto your faith now because your faith and our love would be all that you would need

Instead I watched as you withered and grew weak
Treating you with insipid clichés that had no meaning or honesty to them
I watched placidly and listened without any real emotion whilst your spirit fought a terrible war

You left me a wonderful legacy of stories of sad and happy times
But your legacy is too painful to retrieve
This is my loss.
My regret.

Helen L .Barker

A brief moment

Sadness is a brief moment; the cure is finding true happiness in every form.

Andrew C Brown

Fox

Wearily dragged down by the heaviness of this burden
Drained by being the one to throw it off its scent
Her deliberate stubbornness leads the hound
No attempt to apprehend him he drives his teeth into limb after limb
The fox looks blankly at his Judas and she is appalled by her own lack of willingness to help and sickened by the quivering helpless sight
Legs and arms are ripped along the length of their vow
Blood flow oozes slowly now, jewelled clots heralding ruby celebrations
With the prized brush in sight comes anger and frustration at the lack of life in the once animated man
Despairingly she pities herself only.
It is her life that is now over not his

Helen L. Barker

A Stand for a Fool

I stand and offer my soul to you, hoping that I will be accepted with open heart and a warm smile.

Do not forgive me: I only ask for my life. Do not turn me to the cold dark night: I only wish to warm my sorrow by your fire of passion.
I stand before you like a fool.

"The common dilemma of man!"

Andrew C Brown

The Dark Room

Staring into silvery solutions
I look for clarity: the happiest white immortality
My blurry hazy image has to be covered to be seen
Not smothered but finely coated micron thin.
So I dip with tender touch developing the fine line between high and low but what we find is not the fairytale ending but a distortion of even remotest novel???
Swinging unnaturally between acidic and caustic.
The corrosion devours paper-thin trust and my faith is blotted out by abhorrent hatred of you and I after cruel words had tugged fruitlessly at my veil.

I turned to relief and generosity
Shielded in acceptance the deed had been done regret cannot be the chosen solution
Selfishly I prefer the solitude of the dark room to displaying your cheapened soft focus dream.

Helen L Barker

A Time for glory

I lift my head to look you in the eye, I have come here to ask forgiveness but you fear me. I remained loyal to you. My sword was at your request. I defended your honour. Why have you forsaken me now?

I bow my head in pity, not for myself but for you. I call on my brothers to witness the loyalty here, I ask for your courage and you gave without question, now I ask you to stand before me. Witness this in turn. The honour for our blood, the sacrifice we made was beyond this reward. Look with your eyes see the moment before you, I can ask nothing of you now. I will promise you this: I will not forsake you, I will not drop my sword.

She has betrayed us all with her false promise. I pledged my heart for you. You are my Queen, I see your tears and I hear you weep. I hear your sorrow, I can stand with my head held high, before my men I vow this my Queen, We are mortal men that stand before our God and ask only one thing, that we die with dignity and honour. We demand nothing we stand and fight; we protect the weak, our families, and our land and Our Queen.

We seek no gold or personal wealth; greed or jewels that sparkle do not rule us. Our wealth is honour. We see the jewel sparkle through our children. If you believe in freedom stand before your demon and announce/declaim/proclaim? Your allegiance, do not stand-alone. Command and we will conquer.

In my heart I feel the sorrow, I will not allow another drop of blood to drain from the body of my men, and this sword will no longer cut your enemy. My shield can no longer shelter you from the evil of our enemy. Stand before us, my Queen and denounce your guilt. Do not rule with the hatred of single thought. Believe in our demand and we will deliver with endeavour and we will provide the strength to destroy our foe. In the face of the fires of hell we will drive them. Our mercy will not be kind, I command my men to fight. I lead with hope and we will triumph.

I ask you with my hand before you do not forsake us.

Andrew C Brown

Twelve

Smothered in the ice apron and bitter disappointment she bemoans her aspect
Her arctic iridescent exterior is transparent
Inside a red-hot oven rages it cannot melt the walls of steely grey
As tremors give warnings of a blacker misery
She searches higher but fails to find and expectation is her worst enemy

Frustrated tears are spat out
Salty water that she has cooled into frozen intolerance
She haughtily sculpts the barricade and cuts the supporting rope
The only pact they had recoils slivering snake-like vicious? Hiss as the remains
are freed from any other ties
He can do no other than catch this his only gift
Precisely the whetted cord severs his palms
There's no foothold or grip possible now
Glacial blunt indifference glimpses excruciating ineptness
Jagged edges of flesh spew crimson into the void the blackness pitifully reaches out
to his helplessness

Helen L .Barker

Always plan something

Do not spend all your days thinking about what bad things might happen; just plan your day to make good things happen.

Andrew C Brown

Coracle

From my home-made coracle I look out across the vastness
Jealously sulking at the first affectionate glimpses

Drawn by inherent need, oceans are brought together by joint purpose
Jack-pot winners
Their journey sheds all fears and they dive deeper within themselves to find humility in the purest nutrients
Hungrily they seek out themselves in one another now revelling in the intensity of this passion they rocket skywards breaking into unknown territory
Synchronised but not mechanical, then one after another in ultimate delight and appreciation
Their flock complete they arch effortlessly back into the water

The coracle rocks uneasily until they are gone and the water is calm again

Helen L. Barker

At Last

Searching in a sea of green I find my island in you. The yellow sand that reflects the sun is the blonde hair that falls on my pillow while you sleep.
I feel your heart beat while my head lies on your breast. The warmth of your body wraps my soul in comfort and security.
I hunger for the taste of your lips, that moment when they touch and the passion runs from me to you.

I will always hold you, I will never destroy this.
Only build a world of tranquillity with emotion and warmth. Give me your hand and come with me. Our journey has started. Walk at my side and we face the future together.
A sweet smile in the morning and a kiss good night.
This is our hope and we have come to collect, together we hold our moment in our hands cupped around every drop.

This is my love I share it with you.

Andrew C Brown

Corridor

I sit sodden in tear-stained regulation blue
Absolutely petrified, I can't even lift my head as the footsteps approach.
The hallowed clunk of heels as she approaches
I stand obligingly and mutter "Good morning"
The "What?" rings in my ears and hot tears well but I won't cry again
Specks of violet from my lips fiercely guard what's left of the pot
Trembling I raise my head to meet her eyes
For one second the blackness opens
Amazingly I can see my brilliant blue, but then it's gone forever
Desperate to find our common flag I offer apologies
But the pallid nail scratches piercingly breaking any bond
How did I ever deserve this?
Uninteresting remains get ruthlessly raked and weeded.
Blanched I am ejected to rebuild my rainbow

Helen L. Barker

Dad

Two precious gifts stand side by side, a smile with a cheeky grin. Little sweet eyes that have no sin,

Moments of innocence are what we create. My beautiful children I will not debate.
Each lesson they will learn and how they play, I never will forget this day.
The gentle touch of my daughter's hand my son is playing in the sand
What a pleasure to participate, in my children's game I am eating from a plastic plate.

My son looks around my daughter cannot frown, oh dear what can this be, or is it time for tea.

I only watch and I am in awe I must play horsy on the floor.

I thank you from the bottom of my heart, and it's not all that bad, I just love being a dad.

When they sleep I stand and stare I hope they follow with a little care. My son will grow strong and meek my daughter will be madam of the week

What a gift we have and sure I know I will not like my daughter's first beau!

Grazed knees a simple dab, boy it's great being a dad.

Andrew C Brown

Leaf

A lack of want is all I desire
Not sealed certification
That has failure embossed into it
No defence sees dawn on the horizon and
Belief in his own rhetoric dissipates pathetically
Like butter melting in the sun
Our summer relationship turned rancid
Hidden in the comfort of daily routine
Legendary impulsiveness gives way to reticence
I too spin my thumbs to think
Words form in my head but cannot be extracted they have drowned in a single tear
The mask was ripped and its shreds have long since dissolved
Sense of self, esteem and an entirety publicly denied
What's left of an innocent trust wrapped in the insincerity of normality?
Incoherent thoughts to remedy that situation borne out in a certain outcome
This is one graduation ceremony I'm not pleased to stand
Its finality should herald new beginnings not
Rub rocks of salt painfully deep into wounds
This newfound freedom won't be an end to it
I cannot create the circle
Normality was never to be my chosen path
I have created a twisted tree, its diseased branches stretch into brittleness
Time and again looking for new growth finding only pity or a closed door
Following each to the end searching for just one sign of life
A place to catch my breath and grow
A place to tend a trusting green leaf of my own

Helen L Barker

Dedicated to a Special Friend

I have never met you or had the privilege to stand at you side; your courage comes from your innocence. Each day offers a new beginning and an opportunity to learn a new emotion or make a new friend. How does a mere adult like me find the same courage? You will always create a special time; your presence brings joy to all. Our world offers gratitude and we would feel incomplete without your smile

You offer a spirit that we cannot imagine, how can we repay our moments that you created. A sweet boyish smile and a sudden tantrum. The politeness of a thank you after receiving a treat. The moment when you sleep that special place we cannot go. How do we live to your standard?

The world is open and you have earned the right to walk in and explore without objection, this is your playroom, we enter only as guests.

Our courage falls a league short of yours; you take a journey without complaint and walk in a direction without question.

The purity we handle with dignity, the sadness of our selfishness we fear. Now we show you strength, you provide a feeling of hope for tomorrow. This provides the strength that tells the world you are here, and here you will remain, in our hearts forever. Your light burns the brightest and this brightness shows us the way. Each day is a representation of the power of childhood. For me I have not had the privilege to enter your world but without knowing it you provide me with an inner strength to continue on through each day of pain, if you can do it, so can I. Thank you Reuben.

Andrew C Brown

Moon Walking

He stumbles upwards, pushing decency aside
But the soft ripples of sand crumble beneath his feet
With no firm ground he lurches from one to another unsteadily
Temptingly forbidden he can wait no longer so
To speed his progress he makes a monstrous gesture
Crass strides to satisfy his already whetted appetite
Far ahead he sees the heavenly oasis
A lusty thirst drives him forward. His ambition blinds him to the black vastness directly in his path. He plummets downwards, zigzag against jagged rocks, acutely sharp razor jibes
In realisation he prays for a moonstone death
Instead ripped apart his body smacks against the granite floor
There's no respite in this repose
Still breathing his heart pounds, begging to be released
He turns to look for help but cannot find compassionate forgiving light
Dark despair and gloom cataract his eyes
His body is shrouded by hurt and remorse
This breathing corpse lies until an eternity comforts to an endurable grief
In pinstriped toleration he pockets anguish,
And up he stands
Dutifully and stoically recalling brighter happy times
Hopefulness in tiny sparkling memories makes stars in his night,
He prays to see life's definition and he climbs again
Grasping the rocks once his enemy now his saviour maybe?
He implores a satellite to be his guide, only her reflection can ignite the inner light
But dissatisfaction is cratered into his soul
He finds a bleak desolation to be his landscape
So now numbness: an automatic protective response, unemotional drift
Unable to recognise kindness in any burning spirit
He cynically extinguishes each flame in his vacuumed existence

Helen L. Barker

Dry Your Tears With Love

*Dry your tears with love my darling; we have lost our dreams along the way.
I never thought I would stand in the rain alone; the sweet raindrops hide my sorrow.
And I can no longer dry my tears with love.*

We stand with strength and true emotion; we bind our existence with the fibre of truth and trust.

I stand alone with the memory of you and I wish for my soul to walk at your side. You and I walking in the dark, with our souls apart, our secrets were no longer in each other's mind.

I give you everything, I put myself in your hands, and all I want is to see you in the light. I no longer run from the past.

I need to get beyond this wall, I only wanted to walk from the anger, I could no longer hide in the darkness, everything I am is because of you, Dry your tears with my love, the pain of regret can no longer be my excuse for sorrow.

My illness was my love; I did not search in the open, my hand was here, you placed the spirit and I move in the other direction. Dry your tears with love, and I will dry my tears with sorrow and regret.

I walk alone in the wind, the rain hides my tears and the love will remain in my soul. The sweet memories are all here and they will remain for my entire life. In hope you will reach me, and I will return in spirit. No longer will you dry your tears alone, one day we will try our tears together with love.

Andrew C Brown

Seagulls over Barnsley

They squawk noisily heralding a new independence a loud hailer to my apparent existence more albatross than soaring seagull.
With a capital D I place my right hand on the black book
Horrified by this shock into reality
I read the words like a bedtime story
I'm no longer in that dependant game of charades choosing to sit it out
Here's the first unwanted winning ticket
Oblivious, the clunk of the fill passes me by
Fuel gushes into heady thoughts of nights in and Eleanor-style alter ego beckoning
Keep smiling; crass words from kind people but I no longer mourn this death instead I'm flooded with a relief at the funeral
A saddened heart whirls into the multi-coloured vortex spinning further into the oily dispersion. Puddles emulsify into a lake forcing my hand
Walking away from the grave is the easy part: my comfort is an indefinable heart within the swirl. Lack of self mixes the colours to dirty grey diesel stains
Dipping into it I wonder if I'd ever distil this drowning soul
the vortex turns The Scream into a calm serene landscape and a shining skeletal cast covers all that is done

Helen L. Barker

Embrace

In any triumph, embrace the moment. It does not last forever....
Continue on and progress for a while!!

If you ask me to deliver the moment I will only deliver the past, I can only touch a dream that holds no reality and yet when you ask me I will deny my true emotion.

Do not search my soul; do not seek what stands before you. In a moment of time, reach and follow your road to a destiny of spiritual being and understanding.

Andrew C Brown

The Red Dress

Taking the mantle of the grey lady
High-speed life blurs past
Status upholds their banner of self-importance with credit card feelings
That crumble to dust the second you reach to touch.

The red silk dress will haunt me forever
It is remembered more than I am with cruel comparisons
There was a person in there too.
So, assassinated, the silk lies discarded in a crimson pool

My echo bounces round the cold deserted room
Uncomfortable silences make a mockery of the guest list
A stomach-churning pain is just an empty bag, saggy and lack-lustre
Its purpose gone robbed of its contents by opportunist thieves

But when I sit to commit these thoughts I am rich
I dive into a warm milky bath, free to swim above and below
I can breathe and I can see
I would rather this than anything. I can be me

Helen L Barker

Flat Pack Furniture

It's the weekend; your favourite team is playing at home, the Sunday pint with your mates, the laughter and boyish banter without your contribution. Why did she plan this weekend? It's here, that weekend you have been dreading, it's that trip to the commercial park. DIY in yellow and blue.

It's a wardrobe with matching tables and a mirror that stands by itself. The wife was clear that it had to be. Why can you never get flat pack furniture in your car?
Every Saturday come rain or shine the boots of cars with boxes out of line.
The faces of troubled men, weekends destroyed by instructions written in Swedish, Polish, Chinese and other such languages, possibly more than ten.

Now it's time to face the challenge, with screwdriver, hammer and saw, we open the box, and discover an arrangement of wood metal and other things that look like mechanical components from an aircraft.

Where are the instructions? What do they say, it's so confusing what do I do.
"Right don't panic, just follow the print and diagrams." It can't be too hard!!
Item A fits to item B, using the block set unit attach E to K. Using the screws in box D to attach the frame with the door.

Ok with pencil behind the ear, we begin. Each piece fits in a different place the instructions must be wrong. The wife brings the tea, why is it she knows more about this than me?
With out a thought she comments, add A to C, with the metal holder, put the running rails on the side and attach the frame to E,D and F. Simple!!

How do they know that??
I am now convinced, a woman invented flat pack furniture. It's plain to see. A man would never invent this monstrosity!!!
Why would we want to destroy a perfectly good weekend!!
I wonder how united got on??

Andrew C. Brown

The flag

The flag is tattered and torn
By the savagery of its duty
He pleads with a cool breeze
To warm him and make him fly

The scars are clearly seen
His is a moth-bitten existence
This disfigurement is no perfect foil
And he's folded in the bottom drawer for years

When the mistral calls
The essence of him longs to leap and fly
Primary colours desperate to display
Bursting for any show or use

Without stopping she passes
Right through his heart
Without definition there's no ceremony
No parade without proclamation

Even devastation has been swept away
Just the broken stripes from history
Clumsily pieced together
Back to the drawer, his mausoleum

Helen L. Barker

High Wire Annie

*A warm caring touch traces his finger along my lip line
This single united act is cocooned in a gleaming glass sphere
I put this on the highest pedestal that no one can reach
Such admiration at its crystal reflection
I ache to be the creator of perfection where each piece fits exactly
I marvel the simplicity of this ultimate place
 Inspiring in untold confidence, destiny has a way of getting even
Such inspiration cannot survive reality. To be shone above all other, just once
An ambition galvanised into crumpled used envelopes.
Fate slips a greasy layer between determined cupped fingers
Bolts of rejection force space between skin and sphere
Charred palms so tender yet circus pursuits persist
Maintaining fingernail grasp I edge along the high wire
Crowds gasp in anticipation at the oncoming twang as excited waves shiver along the thin black line as I steady my balance. Why can't I see the impending shock waves?
Intuition used to be my best friend passing through the heart like lightning
I'm blinded on my lofty trapeze as obvious sheets of bright white define a moment
The prism is universally viewed in the momentary splendour
Then, as is its destiny, smashes into the floor
A million shards of glass each one a constant reminder of rebirth marks a hideous deformity. Picking up the pieces is the new occupation. Is this recognition that I seek with a silver dustpan? The wax has been allowed to set
Normality is stranded by a canyon too deep to measure or conceive
 I can create the mountain of optimism but cannot heal this cavernous rift
An image not even half empty could drain the ocean drawing intimacy from its coveted source, but sapped of energy now, I no longer care nor want to try
Sickened by my own pathetic insignificance and reliance in others
In a Pattern of function without true purpose
I resolve to shield a timid flicker with the concentration of maverick thought*

Helen L. Barker

How to Write Poetry

Search deeper and you will find the emotion to support your pen when it rapes the paper with pure passion, anger, hatred and at the same time delivers a sweet innocence, captured in treasured moments we call memories.

Andrew C Brown

The Coconut

Force of the swing breaks the wax seal & they turn to face one another
In one anxious moment their faces are just breaths apart...
In her grey-blue he has seen a longing to be accepted, to be truly desired
He has heard the bare inner voice, intimate beyond usual comprehension
He has touched her healing not with caresses but inquisitive prods
Drawn from a hidden well, painting words with its waters
Monochrome thoughts are pressed into delightful multicolour for the first time.
A single bewildered tear of insignificant disappointment is shamefully dissolved
In an ocean of sorrow and horrific grief of the thousands, she holds onto tiny podgy hands and gratefully thanks God as a whole universe of all that matters to one is a non-entity to another. final chapters turn pages of inevitability and stranded she's left to look upwards
In his icy-blues there's a gleaming shiny curtain. However on closer inspection carelessly drawn and snagged cloth reveals the scene beyond
The fisherman without his bait sits straight-backed
He has fashioned a barbed hook from angry exchange. A successful catch but at a despicable price. Experience has woven a splendid net of ambition, wealth, status Held at every corner by false testimony and insincerity
Entirely ineffectual as faith, honesty and a true self slip away
the yield is loneliness, dissatisfaction and a frustration that only contempt, selfishness and greed can cover.
Upon celestial throne he's crowned in concentrated achievement
illuminated by the moon he can fly his net across the skies
Boundless performance, he moves to more consequential subjects
without reliance he can do anything he pleases
Halting the reverse action she stands pushing down hard on small pedals determination focused into the gravity of adult responsibility, facts and targets but spinning her thumbs in circles wonders in awe at the starry skies
what impact, if any, this satellite really made

Helen L. Barker

I Forgot the Rain

*Look and listen, we have been here before.
Search through the litter to find the empty script you wrote
The words mean little and do not reflect a true man
If I can be a better man will you believe the fairy tale?
I only stood in the rain and forgot who I was.
Lost in this everlasting darkness with small incandescent light*

*I only had anger for lunch, but I promise to have love for dinner
Come and see what stands before you. The illness eats away at my broken heart
I search into the millennium and find the truth in all the bright colours
Please come and join me, the water remains blue.
I hope to see you at the party and find our common ground
Did I say I was sorry or did I just forget?*

*We will feel all our moments in this gospel we call emotion. All our emotions come with price tags. When we need them they are not there, when we don't need them they have taken over our very own circle. We are pushed in all directions, we run through the rain but still we get wet form the pure water drops that soak and hide our tears.
I remain sober; no longer do I run from little demons that spin my mind. I did not forget the rain; I went outside and just got soaking wet.*

Andrew C Brown

The Alchemist

Instilled into the air is a fragile thread
So entangled, the diamond centre is a goal denied.
Working in reverse the knot is pulled tighter
Until new thought is fashioned from unseen vulnerability.
Tradition turned on its head
Carefully injected fear highlights imperfections.
A propensity for real purpose so intense
It enduringly binds heart & soul
Until this stranded idea is understood
And myth becomes reality
Beyond comfort encouragement is jet powered
And fuelled imagination rockets skyward
This uncertain alchemist has created golden flecks from charcoal
A revolution whose gentleness belies its science.
Formulated ideas achieve a different level of consciousness
Achievable warmth glows optimistically
As conjecture deemed too fanciful
Strides from puddles into oceans.
Continuity exasperated onto frozen pages
Melts myopic thought with newfound clarity.

Helen L. Barker

If

If you stand before me, remember to judge me for tomorrow and not for yesterday.
If you reach out your hand, I will hold it and look forward.
If you see me cry don't pity my tears.
If you see only anger in my heart look beyond
If I stand before you and ask for forgiveness don't turn me away
If I ask for your love I will ask in pure truth and with a sincere heart
If I tell you I am sorry, it's not just words
If I pray before God I pray with a heavy heart, my knees will bleed with guilt but I will not stand to relieve the pain.
If I ask for my punishment I will accept it without question, this is a small price to pay.
If we are forced in directions, we may not want to go
If I return and stand before you again look into my heart and only see what is good.
If you stand before me look beyond my pain see the truth in me.
If you ever forgive me do not forgive me in sorrow
If you reach me my soul will belong to you
If you find me I will no longer be lost
If I had loved you all this would not exist.

Andrew C Brown

Learning to Swim

My dreams are made of fantastic worlds
Where boundaries have no definition
Experiences too happy to contemplate
By taking courage in my own self
I can put myself in this magical place
Where I am twinned with contentment
Connected to a happiness I will never want to let go

Haltering (faltering?), one foot begins to wade into warm water
I cling childishly to romantic notions
Singly covered in bravado that Shelley would despise
So coaxed gently by strong hands
I'm led out to mix and mingle
Surprisingly easy I'm
Elevated to a place unable to recall this freedom

Helen L. Barker

Journey by Taking the First Step

We drift from one suitcase to another with no sense of direction; we search for a place that offers completeness with no complication.

This place we know but we can only search, we look through time and beyond. We explore through memory and moments. In reality the moment is with us, in reality we have explored this place.

We did not understand or even see the talent this place could offer. Blindness was our illness, with eyes that focus on simple trinkets of meaningless substance without a value.

I can only walk in one direction without detour or side steps; the journey will only direct me. If I choose to walk, hold my hand and walk with me. Tomorrow we begin another journey

Andrew C Brown

Shopping Days

A warmth had wrapped itself around them
Binding the vow of growing old together
Nothing more and no one else.

Remembering the first shared smile
He swings overcoat with familiar gait
And he makes his way through daily chores

Once an intrusion to life now his mainstay
Polite enquiries countered with "mustn't grumble"
He steps back out into the cold

Bowing his head to fall back to a private world
Treasured times have faded like sepia frames
He journeys, waterlogged, with tears of sadness

At 22 his heart felt intensely full and content
Bequeathed with love, the golden era over forever
But only a beat apart, she still follows him home

Helen L. Barker

Look Through the Window

Sitting in my favourite chair looking through the window, watching the world drift by in seasons of bloom, cold and warmth.
I wonder at the marvel of life, each step passed my window the child that walks to school becomes the adult that walks to work.

My favourite chair reflects the beauty, the residue beyond the glass of my window. I stand and look at the moments of expression. They are only moments but each moment makes a time, each time is a life. I have only simple words to describe my silky feelings.

I have no hypocrisy; my sincerity stands by the dignity of a fine oak tree that has stood the test of time. I look through the window and stand by the fountain of inspiration. The water reaches my soul and I am pushed into clear thinking. I stand by my window and watch. I am honoured to view the marvel of each day. The vases of red tulips brighten the room, a room of family memories. A room of security, the walls have seen so many moments, a sweet cuddle with a child of blonde. A word of encouragement before the door opens to the big wide world.

I look though the window and wait for the next day with the complete enthusiasm of life. Today we begin again. Maybe I should say thank you.

Andrew C Brown

A kiss

The most intimate thing
And yet the most trivialised act
A tidal wave of urgent and passionate
Gentle and tender true feeling lay bare
Shamefully easy to receive
But with all your heart a precious gift

Helen L. Barker

Love at the Table

When you criticise do it with modern philosophy, if you sound like a pirate I will pull you in and rip your mind from a skull of confusion.

The purple of the kitchen table, the bowl of fruit was missed in a crystal shape, the touch of little fingers grasp the pure red of the apple, each crunch released the moisture of taste.

We all sit at the table and eat in silence; each potion has a distinctive flavour. The smell from the kitchen as each serving finds its way to the table on plates of gold. That tantalising aroma of spice and fresh ingredient, what more could we ask for?

Please sit at my table eat from the selection and do not feel obliged to repay. I offer the delight with friendship and warmth. This is your table and I welcome you, I cannot refuse.

It is only the true emotion that dissolved our well being, if you sit at my table leave your sword in the cold. Drink from the goblet of pearl and feel the nectar of the wine. It tastes sweet, this is my love for you and the food is my security to provide.

Join me and think not of yesterday only of tomorrow!

Andrew C Brown

Octopus

She stretches out to reach
Clammy tentacles envelop us
Relentlessly tirelessly mercilessly squeeze tighter
No speaking or moving are allowed
We are robbed of gestures that belie our emotion
Wide-eyed fear as we face a last breath
We see line and now would willingly step over it
Our final steps like our first, a triumph of independence

Helen L. Barker

Old and Forgotten

The old woman is still, she has no movement; her entire life came to an end when the final breath escaped from her body. Each moment of time runs by, no one will call today. Her body remains in a still shade, her soul long gone; maybe she has companionship, a special friend who went before, and a loved one from time gone by. A secret love, which could not be spoken. Capturing a moment in an isolated time, with no prying eyes, no scandal or shameful jest.

In life we ignore, we do not spend the time for sharing we learn nothing. We remain lonely in the arena of personality.
The letters in a red ribbon, each page talks of love.
"The moment you touched me I tingle with anticipation. I want you; I feel your body next to mine. The warmth you provide protects me from the cold!"

How could this be, each word written talks of sociable momentum? Where did this love go? It will remain in words on paper tied in a red ribbon. The letters remain still next to the old women.
The black and white picture in a frame of leather, somebody else's man, maybe a father with the possibility of a grandchild or two. The handsome rugged face of her true love.

Her life had become empty with heartache and loneliness, never to be replaced. The feelings of his touch remain in the deepness of her mind. How she longed for his meritorious company. He dwindled away a long time ago.

Life continued in a vacuum of existence. The supermarket aisle provides the simulation of a particular day. No eye contact or conversation. On the most memorable occasion a moment of self-pity, a small act of kindness. Each long night waiting for the morning to bring a repetitive day, the purpose of life lost in sheer sadness.
The body remains still, maybe tomorrow someone will call, and maybe the supermarket aisle will miss the simple steps that pass by the cornflakes.

Andrew C Brown

Radio Frequency

Her hands are long and rounded and freshly pink
Plump glowing healthily with a light touch
These are windows to her soul
Presses against the glass to hear her acceptance
But radio frequencies with muffled bass notes block out senses
Impounded by the glass she cannot hear nor feel or touch her emotion
Forever skirting merrily round the apron speaking incessantly
Never actually saying anything
Desperately wanting to stretch each inquisitive finger into history
Loving and caring and sharing
But finding only cold stony glances
A lifeless response to dull what's left of humour, enthusiasm or hope
In anger frustrated fists curl and bray onto the panes
Instead of breaking the glass futility grips so tightly
She fights to breathe imploding silently
The only sign fat hot tears

Helen L. Barker

Part of You

When you sleep the world spins in silence, when you sleep I watch in truth. I search your very existence, searching for a way in, so I can share the freedom you have, to feel as you do.
I search for the reason of you; each day when you wake, the inner world begins. The moment you open your eyes life begins again. Each day I fall for you, each day is a new paradise in your arms, when you wake I look into your eyes.

You are the flower that catches the raindrop, you are the summer meadow that echo's tranquillity and lazy peaceful Sunday afternoons.

In a moment you sleep: in a moment you will drift in to another world I cannot go. I will sit by your side and enter your dreams through my own sleep. My spirit will encourage your mind to drift into a new world and together we will share our lives in pure innocence and true happiness with no room for darkness. We will not have unpleasant memories only new beginnings. Each part of you will develop in me, I can only stand and admire this soul that stands before me.

If I speak I can only communicate in my own mind, which does not translate the true part of my inner feelings for you. I watch you sleep and I still search for the door that will allow me to enter your heart and lose myself in a sweet pool of emotion, love and the enjoyment of life.

In any moment of time the demand and quest for life is so powerful. The strength that surrounds you is beyond any boundary. I look through the wire fence lost in whirlpools of sweetness. I dive in and soak up the moment. At last I am content. This is you. Without compromise or sadness your very existence is my meaning. Your quest for my contentment is endless.
I will remain in this positive state. The ocean will drift and the tide of time will not alter the nature of who you are and what I have become. With this, I can only say, I Love You!

Andrew C Brown

Friendship

At Christmas my house of many rooms
Is empty bleak and robbed of most possessions
They fill but one room
So I furnish with what remains
Something that burns within
An everlasting flame
That cannot be extinguished
Cannot be stolen or destroyed
Created caringly from skilled craftsman
I call my friends
Nurtured by loving memories
Over time kindled into fireside homeliness
Of loyalty and trust
No fear of showing the true colours of the flicker
I give to you my gift of love
My friendship

Helen L. Barker

Past on a Stage.

If you dream about the past you will never enter the future
The footsteps that fell behind you can never be retraced, turn and face backwards to look at the end of my beginning.
If I walk forward I have the handrail of life to support me in times of misconception and fear.

In the bleakest moment I face the future with my mind in raven black. I search my soul for the courage to provide strength and guidance. I have a purpose. I walked with the wizard of my dreams. He told me of the oak tree with the deep roots that held fast in times of prevalence.

I come to the stage to act out my dream, the floorboards creak and the applause has a warm tone. The audience is my world of familiar faces. I take the bow and accept the appreciation from the crowd as the flowers fall at my feet I reach to the warmth of the applause my arms open and ready to receive the love. Tomorrow I will read the critics and the comments will be made in truth or lack of understanding.

At least I do not run back into the past, I face only in forward direction, regardless of critic.

Andrew C Brown

Tramp

In the alley he sits amongst the bins
Remnants of yesterday's news is his carpet
A feeble warmth gained from the last drops
Of a discarded can
Haziness culls any feelings of sorrow
What's left just a craving for a never ending blackness
Searching skies for signs of comfort
No angelic friend this night

Helen L. Barker

Pink and Warm

Have you entered here to dream of fairy tales?
Do you search for truthful meaning in dark always?
I have a feeling that you have been here before
You drink until you stand on the floor and move with uneasy feeling
How can we stand before you, I will not offer you my soul and you will not take it
How the shape falls from the sand in the hourglass is incredible, the grain has a uniformed presence each grain topples from the top to the bottom.

If you touch my heart with your fingers I will offer a quite silence in a blanket of elegance, but remember this: I was a demon and you walk a fine line
I will walk in willow lane with the scent of the trees and the decent odour is caught on the gentle wind. The pollen floats on air with a feeble lightness, no gravity to pull the moment back to brown shade of the earth.

I have been here before, I hope you will come with me, take my hand let your fingers wrap with mine we will have a pinkness and I will feel warm.

Andrew C Brown

India

Smile for the camera
In any other setting!
My pity is misplaced
In the holiday album
As grinning inanely
In a back drop
Not of lights and shutters
But gutters of filth and hunger
A fine career of begging
Regalia of rags
In these days
Of obscenity that sickens
My only comfort is
A feeble thing
These friends have nothing
But each other

Helen L. Barker

Reach in Darkness

In my dreams, my world is dark.
In my dreams, my world is despair
In my dreams, sadness falls in place of light.
In my dreams, I reach into the darkness, searching for the warmth of a gentle hand.

To reach in darkness without vision is like walking into the hell of fear, in darkness fear is all you have. I will reach beyond that fear;
I will find the warmth of a gentle hand.
I will walk through the darkness and beyond.
In my dreams I can only achieve.
In my dream I can only reach out.
In my dreams I can see beyond all darkness.
In my dreams you came to me and offered your hand, you found me in the darkness.
Now my darkness is warmth, and in my dreams I am always warm.

Andrew C Brown

Red Wine Friends

This sun has caused a catalytic reaction
In early stages the transformation curve radiates
Exponentially as an uncontrollable closeness ensues
An uncertain world to fidget in the limelight
But with this display untouched feeling is poured
My senses love this liquid momentum
His red wine glass full to the brim reflects in mine
Hoarsely attempting to voice opinion seems futile
A cheeky grin in another league would be game set and match
A quiet but growing confidence in my newfound friend
Pours another glass of wine

Helen L. Barker

Remember

To stand and listen but hear no sound.
To look at the buildings and only imagine with no understanding.
Each post and fence has a secret of evil to tell.
To stand and listen and feel the moment, to stand and smell the fear and senselessness.
This home to terror looks helpless and non-significant now.
I stand in each room with my eyes open wide and my heart running fast. We find it so hard to believe.

If we forget we have not learned. If we repeat we stand in pure ignorance.
I ask you to close your eyes and feel the torment and suffering, feel the fear, absorb the sounds and moments falling into hopelessness, deep pools of despair and islands of sacrifice where admiration is beyond worthiness.
A child cries a mother protects, the haunting silent screams that cannot be heard by a distant world.

This place remains evil; it stands as a reminder of the evil we have created as human beings. The complete untouched cruelty that only the human mind can develop without a meaning or a reason.
This place is the manufacture of sorrow, death and disgust. Do not forget the mounds of property, each bundle has its own personal belonging. A suitcase, a pair of shoes, my grandmother's hairbrush.

Each item once was owned by the joy of life, Walk in silence, pay some respect, you no longer suffer, your life becomes a purpose, do not forget, remember this place. When you feel. Remember the smell; remember the rooms and that terrible place were so many people walked into the life of peace. Remember life that is a gift, it has a purpose. We only come to look and try to imagine. We cannot feel like they did we cannot experience that time. I kneel and ask for forgiveness, it seems fruitless but I offer my sorrow to all who have suffered here. I will always remember.

Andrew C Brown

You Wrote This

So long, she has cradled in her hands her precious self
Not gently, as you or I would on an open hand
But pressed tightly shut to fiercely protect from further mocking bruises

In a moment out of character her grip loosens showing
a tiny jewelled chalice, encrusted with kindly gems:
Loyalty, honesty and love; bar-coded between steel fingers.
Putting this chalice on a cushion requires more courage than a world leader.
To endure a procession of passing tourists,
To be publicly open to criticism is a daring act of art.
But this is life.
Only by risking a delicate state of self for one lone compliment
Will she find a loving friend

Helen L. Barker

Remembering Love

*Remember a moment in time, this moment must be powerful with strong emotional content. Close your eyes and feel the moment.
Imagine the smell, the feelings and the condition of your heart.*

In each case you will only remember love. You will feel love, which is surrounded by complete warmth. This warmth invites you to explore without fear or sadness.

To venture in with open heart and mind, for me this is a place I dream of, I search each day following omens and clues of life. Searching for hidden answers to questions that have no wonder or meaning.

Each road I take has a thorny path; with each step my feet bleed, with each step the pain runs through my heart. This pain causes the sadness to disrupt the reality of the journey through life.

Love has a power beyond our understanding, but this lack of understanding does not create fear or weariness, it's inviting and welcomes you with open arms. You fall and land with secure comfort; your soul is wrapped in pure softness. That softness cushions your heart protects it from cruelty but asks no reward.

*Be loyal to your heart, follow your dreams, reach out for the chances that seem to avoid you. Search for true happiness.
But always remember a moment in time, this moment must be powerful with strong emotional content.*

Andrew C Brown

9-5

He is frustrated by her blindness
In her own lack of self worth
And irritated that any growing dependence will
Problematically disrupt his expected life style
With relief, he steps back into 9-5 limelight

In her eyes he is a shining fated star
Drawn to channel energy defined in inspiration
She confidently weaves each line with well chosen adage
Without a muse, hers are threadbare thoughts
That even a fisherman's knot can't hold

Helen L. Barker

Running Through Tunnels

Running through tunnels chasing specks of light just focusing on the horizon. Each side of me is shadowed in a pitch black.
Only looking up, running towards the light. The noise echoes all around as you run through the dark. The only direction you can follow is the way ahead, no left or right up or down. Keep running forward follow the light.

In all this blackness I see no way round, I must keep moving forward, do not turn back. The light is getting bigger with every step I take, now I can feel the warmth and the brightness burns my eyes with glory.
My anguish fills my body; my anticipation of hope with majesty awaits my exit.
The light has a meaning and burns in the centre of the universe. All that is good spreads through darkness, ripping away at roots of despair and disorder. Each tentacle of light dissolves the anarchism and rebellion of futile disgust.

The final effort launches me into the arms of security the warmth wraps and cradles me into the hammock of inner sanctuary. I rest in pools of emotion and the wall of strength surrounds my innocence, virtue and purity. Nobody can return me to the tunnel.

I have arrived; I am in the security of my father's arms. With eyes of blue I look at everyone and say in a loud voice. "This is my daddy!"

Andrew C Brown

Friends

Living in a world of least resistance
Juggling the clubs of a daily existence
My circus is filled with a friend's melting pot
Waiting to catch what I cannot

Helen L. Barker

Searching

I am lost in the power of your existence, how can I escape this void?
I look for the door to take me to my destiny, searching for a moment; I feel no truth I am only here because I chose not to be.
I am mortal and vulnerable to all the human emotions that run the parade of life.
I ask for nothing and I came with little illusion of beauty and I know I wish all the memories would leave, the front door is open and I do not stand in the way. I ask you to leave. I am lost for the sake of being lost.

I do not ask for my feelings, I do not ask for this way, it happened with no warning. I ask you to think of me in heaven, I have only the sweet loyalty of my well-being. If I ask you to turn back would you?? I am only a man who has no meaning of understanding. You are my lady and I was a man. If I stand down from my duty please take this as my forgiveness.

I am lost in a soul of madness I am no longer in control of my emotions I have lost my will, it does not matter I am only a man; we made the difference between the two ways. I search my land for my way of life, can I stand alone or do I let it go? Young in all the ways of discovery I ask for my soul to direct the play, search the school yard for all the answers, we are only children, we stand with candles that burn with little protection from the evil that commands the street life we find ourselves in. If I ask this of my direction, I need the wisdom of knowledge, if I knew what I know now, Happiness would be my only companion. The journey has been a long and hard progression. I rest for a while by the stream, I carry too much pain, and if I could forgive myself I would. In my moment I went to Turkey, in the dark by the sea, who asked me for my mercy, I can only ask for some truth, I can only hold onto mercy for a little time…..

Please forgive me; I ask you, do not punish me, I was holding on to mercy for myself. In the deepness (depths?) I found the way to reach the stars. I called out for mercy; I can no longer hold to the truth, I am lost in this mercy. Please forgive me, I should have never have asked you to take the burden. Please forgive me.

My search has come to the end; I am still listening to my favourite song.

Andrew C Brown

His Devotion

For an eternity he would stand in a field of springtime flowers
In each single hopeful bouquet there's an entirety of devotion.
His only requirement an acknowledgement of an ordinary existence
His dream: to gaze into the crystal vase
And magically create perfume from rose petals

Helen L. Barker

Sit for a While

Please sit for a while, remember a moment, cast your mind into a direction where you remember a smile.

Sit for a while and remember the good and bad times we had.

Smile when you remember a memory that made us laugh.

Remember our tears and pain. Remember the truth, the happiness and the bond that held us together.

Sit for a while and share a tear, think only good of me, do not drown in self-pity or anger. Sit for a while and close your eyes drift into memories of pleasure, that morning we played in the crisp snow, the coldness of our breath, the laughter that comes from enjoying the life we have.

Sit for a while and remember the day we argued over nothing, the things we said in moments of dissatisfaction, they are memories that we fear the most, but remember words we spoke were said in moments of anger and carry no meaning.

Sit for a while and remember me, I will always be with you, I will never leave your heart, sit for a while and remember me,

Daddy sit for a while and forget the pain, sit for a while and think of me.

Andrew C Brown

Doves

Each has sought a solace in the other
A quiet contentment settles over the dovecote
With an Astaire-like elegance wings are fanned around their beating heart

This is no place to squander time
A majestic energy of its own is born
Driving an endless search to please

A knowing that each dusk flight
Is not impeded but encouraged
Further journeys distance into unknown lands

Brilliant white softens to a peachy glow
Unforgotten purpose sinks gently on their bed of feathers
And a peaceful drift is theirs

Helen L. Barker

Surround

The moment I look into your eyes, I drift away to a place I call harmony.
In this place I feel only good, evil remains on the outside.
The emotional wellbeing of peace and love.
The touch is warm and kind; petals of red surround me.
The sweet scent of love saturates the air I breathe. The calmness has come, it protects me like my mother's arms.
This place is love
The true meaning of love is here.
But where am I?
This is an easy question to answer
I am lying by your side.

Andrew C Brown

The Metronome

A gentle persistence consistently ticks
Not distracted by nightly brick-walled silences
Nor conversations waltzing in self pity.
Humour is teased thread by thread
Tediously slow progress hindered by
An iron curtain of loneliness within the crowd.
A confusion of fear and misery loop around the roundabout of jumbled voices
A sympathetic supporting hand outstretched is angrily and resentfully dismissed.

But this persistence doesn't leave me.
There, in the background, the hand remains.
In a stronger moment, an easier time, a chance taken lets me hear the tick
A lit candle shows me a way to bed & The Black Panic begins to dissipate.
At last! To eat, to smile and to sleep.
I can see into the beginning of a new day
I put gratitude into words of love, considering my friends, their actions.
I pray my deeds one day lead to their contentment

Helen L. Barker

The Ashtray of Life

I stay for a while and continue with no direction, I am not looking for you. I want to find you again, but I can't look for you.
I am completely lost in this very meaning, why is only the question. Self-pity can be my answer.
If you stand and look, what do you see? Like a glass of red wine, I stand in dark light. The colour is rich and the taste is divine. Drink too much and you will feel the consequence.

If you come to me, ask any question and I will answer, I am free with my emotion.
If I could only reach you. Just look at me, see the whole truth, it stands before you. I have completed my anger. I have forgotten the past, I will remember only the time we had, the time we smiled. The time we cried because the movie was sad.

I am in the ashtray and I can no longer run away. I ask for a little sympathy. I did not mean my life. I ask that you see the consequence of all my pain. If I can return and empty the ashtray, I would. If I call in the shade, will anyone hear me? If I reach out with my open heart, will anyone care?

Today we sit on a bench and watch with no expression, we do not exist here. We sit but the time has stopped for me.

I am in two lives, who am I? Please give me the answer, let me search the truth. If I stay, I will be like the ashtray, one day someone will empty me. The stale smell will linger no more, the spray of perfume will hide the memory. I want to search for you. You never intended to stay with me. In a time and place the love can live freely. I will wait for you. The ashtray has been emptied.

Andrew C Brown

The Oarsman

Between gasps of pain the blurred image looms bigger
A regular swish and flow as oars draw nearer
I am afraid and scurry deeper into tangled thorns and blackness

Giant hands find these cuts and bruises
Scooping me gently from my prickly sanctuary
I'm tended with great care and compassion
Moments numbly pass between day and night until
Yet again I feel warmth and yearn to see home

The ache is a selfish development grown from a selfless act
With physical pain banished the loving cocoon is tapped open.
My ambition realised in a meeting of warmth and crisp excitement
The pale blue is irresistibly attractive
So my elated farewell soars into familiar territory
Writing a glorious freedom across my skies

Happy tears remain
In the hands of love
That let me fly again

Helen L. Barker

The Cottage by the Lake

The true spirit runs with the wind as we sit on the mountain
His eyes reflect the ruggedness of isolated moments wandering the mountains
Sitting on the rock unaware of the hardness and we watch the loch with a distinctive water of colour grey. The rain falls with a refreshing coldness as each drop is absorbed into the material of tweed.

The shades of green and the brown of the fern reflect the dullness of blue with dark clouds. The sinister look of strength and the unawareness of the cold as it beats at the face.
I watch the dark secrets of a man who knows all in a mind of isolation, he tells me nothing but he does direct me away from turmoil. He has my respect he never earned it I gave it without question.

The lane invites me to the warmth of the cottage by the lake; the fire offers a welcome like a thick overcoat. I sit and milk the comfort of my surroundings. I am safe, and the thickness of the soup heats the hunger that burns in my stomach.

Today is a good day I am privileged to enter this domain in a single character. The yellow of the fire provides a light that reaches each corner, following the contours of the room. This is a safe haven full of strength. The cold world remains outside and always will.

Andrew C Brown

The Bag Lady

My paradise is owned by none
Not a glittering gold purse
Nor tangible array of possessions
But a collection of happy times
Crammed into plastic bags
A collage of priceless moments
Greed, mistrust & selfishness
See nothing and are left without
To traipse the streets alone

My paradise is a calm
That sets fingertip links
Into the fossil of you
My want is sated
My soul is pacified
An easy home is ours
For safe-keeping
My paradise is a memory
Of just being with you

Helen L. Barker

The Curtain Falls

If I had to I would let it go, if you do not turn and you ignore the effort it would be a crime.

Never believe each time of anger: it only lasts but one single moment. Behind the thin wall sits a grey old man. He has no purpose he just sits. How can he remind the little boy not to forget his tobacco?

It has no real meaning: only you add the flavour that will improve and satisfy your hunger with shots of protein to boost your need. My energy will provide for you and my stupidity will fade. The balance of who I was, and what I needed will surface to take the final bow, but the audience may not be there when the final curtain comes down. The silent handclap from the balcony. A single audience, no fame for you. Learn the script and re-visit the play. I have a feeling this could be your day!!

Andrew C Brown

The Composer

Sitting at her platform
Awaiting the inspiration train
There's a rush for seats
When it comes,
Skilful formation of
Fine bone china keys
Each a new ticket
An open heart
Playing melodies of sorrow
Just another fragile statistic
Along the line

Helen L. Barker

The Market Place

In the market place you can see so many different things, the hustle and bustle of everyday life continuing, some slow, some not so very slow, and those who travel at light speed. But imagine if you could go beyond the surface of outside life and look within the very framework of our existence. Looking beyond the outside colours, looking into the mysterious and secret lives that we all lead.

Travelling through the minds of individuals, searching for truths and trying to unlock and understand the mentality that divides us to our ambitious existence. Routing out dark sides and locked away memories that damage the very fabric of the life they have affected.

In the market place, the colour is visual and through the viewfinder of the mind we can absorb the spectrum of colours, we can develop our imagination to reflect the colour of our very existence.

To stand in the market place, you are in the vicinity of vocal noise that rotates around the vocabulary of language, the noise of communication, like all forms of reality we only communicate what we say not what we think.

To stand and communicate with your eyes is for greater than the noise of sounding vocabulary that mis-guides and does not direct.

The market place is here every day, next time do not pass by. Stay awhile, see the very moment you are in, and hold that moment and time will stand still in memories and visual awareness. The market place is the place to be.

Andrew C Brown

Puzzle

Somewhere in the fragments I call my mind I see a jigsaw puzzle
Disjointed
Patched together by childish aptitude
I can see clearly the landscape
Almost touch its hedgerow
As the haymaker winds his way through the stream
But my quandary of the final bale
Dissatisfied by my view
I look and see an incompleteness
Can you search sofa and chair for the missing piece?

Helen L. Barker

The Old Man

*He sits in silence watching the world go by
The hardness of the park bench worries him not
How can he worry about something so trivial?*

*His eyes are deep and dark the stare of a man who only exists day by day.
His company is loneliness; the sadness has ripped away the goodness of sweet happy memories*

He suffers in silence, so he does not offend. His feeling of love compassion and dignity lost in the pit of despair.

Each day he kneels at his wife's side, they chat for a while, he arranges the bloom. They will remember a pleasant memory of time gone by. He laughs and most times cries in silence hoping that no one will see the tear roll from his cheek on this cold morning. He will be back tomorrow. He departs with the words, "I love you my darling! I wish you were still here!"

Is this new life?

Andrew C Brown

In the Sand

*Dig deep and scoop handfuls
As, at your side, a closed door remains
Desperately I search through the grains
To unlock what science cannot*

*A slick procession through my fingers
Each a treasured happy time
To find the one to trigger recognition
What could be the key?*

*Resignation to an impotent being
Or are you still behind the door
Selfishly we hope you are
But pray you are not*

Helen L. Barker

The Power of a Minute

The power of one minute can be the difference between life or death, the decisions we make take only seconds but the outcome will develop into whatever it requires. We search for time in all the wrong places, when we find our time we do not spend it wisely. We disregard time as if it is not important.

We consider time to be too short, or in some cases too long, but time is life. Time measures life. Life is our time, during this time we will create, destroy, love, hate. We will begin and end. Our time will allow us to construct our emotions. We will feel pain; happiness, sadness and we will remember good and bad.

Our time is small compared to overall time; it is a tiny second that will pass by with such speed. One day we will only be a memory, in time itself we will become ancestors. Our time is a gift, how we use that gift is our choice. What is certain is we cannot reverse time, we cannot change time gone by, but we can develop future time. We can spend it wisely with many ingredients such as compassion, kindness and above all love. Time allows us to love. Time allows us to share.

Take your time and spend it wisely my friend, time has no walls or boundaries, time is not a box, you can cram and create as many memories as you wish, time allows us this privilege. Reach out and touch the time of others, their time may be shorter than yours. Laugh and be happy as much as you can in time. Time is for living; do not waste it with sadness or hatred. It will lead to a waste of time

Spend time, create memories in time, look back on your time and do not regret any moment. You can only do this if you are prepared to change your tomorrow. Time is our meaning, time is for you and all mankind, take as much time as you can, this is your right and allow yourself time. "Spend your time with love, share your time" The power of a minute has no time.

Andrew C Brown

Hugh

Servitude is my born right
As luxury is to him.
Pomposity created
With the tied cravat,
Arrogance displayed in
A top corner pocket,
Proper and right
Belittle naive honesty
And play the
Mocking jester
To any appreciative audience.

I despise not the serf
But the despot
Bathing in unicorn's milk.
He'd killed the last mammoth
For golden opportunity.
Or grasped Iago's dagger
To further ambition.
Anticipating his future: just
A pillar of salt
How can such narcissisms
Be glorified so?

Helen L. Barker

The Short Journey

Sometimes we plan a journey, it may not have a purpose or a direction, but we plan and leave with the hope of having an adventure. We cannot plan for every eventuality but in my luggage I carry all that I need.

Maybe we will meet special friends!!

Andrew C Brown

The Day Ahead

Fleeting intensity moves from room to room
Looking for a window in an underground house
Distracted thoughts dip into a file marked you.
Hazy days of toxic smoke
I inhale this accustomed environment.
Each door-less room has become the norm.
Ill-judged reasoning toys with existence
Till Chance meets my fumbling.
In the clarity of a porthole
The glass magnifies reality tenfold
Presenting suffocation as the obvious outcome

Bare hands push pebble from pebble
My spirit forces boulders aside
Supremacy of faith beyond my sight
Moves into automatic.
Nails scratch frantically until daylight shines
Uncovering a crushed but breathing being
My beached and bruised soul stands again
To look at the day ahead

Helen L. Barker

The Sweet Cherry Blossom

In a wilderness I look at the wonder, I cannot hide the pain, I cannot hide from my poor soul, I search in the place that has become my very own wilderness.

Like a screaming torment you drive me to the centre of my existence. I cannot find the door; I search through corridors, endlessly searching for my spirit. Do not call my name, do not weep by my stone, you have earned the right to be difficult in an open box.

If you remember me, do not feel the moment with deepness, just smile and remember a smile, it was the beginning, the moment to share and remember the cherry blossom, it was dancing in the wind. The sweet dreams and the smell of the flower will be treasured in time, and no longer will we dance in sorrow.

Andrew C Brown

Without Friends

Without friends
Fragments of a backbone
Form only an arch.
Depression lower than limbo dancer
No longer daylight between
No longer brilliant blue.
Futility of a way forward
As sadness sticks steadfastly.
Heaviness exhausts all attempts
Until our helping hands link
Focussing energy into the sealed lock.
Our bond surrounds you.
A circle of happiness: to be,
To live and to love.

Helen L. Barker

The WAR is Over

I walk from the battlefield with no emotion; I see the torment and the destruction. I see the eyes; they look at me with fear and no meaning of love. I think of home and cry for my soul. I cannot search myself, I wanted to be free. I needed to walk away and face my journey home.

I look into my hands and ask for my forgiveness, I no longer feel clean or human. I have no purpose. I walk from the battlefield and do not look back. I feel the burning of destruction in my back. I walk towards home. What happens behind me does not concern or reach me. My journey takes me to the road home. I want to sleep, with darkness. I will sleep with no dreams; my nightmares will come in time.

I will remember all my actions and I ask that my judgement is fair and without the revolution of hatred. If I stand before you please see the man, do not see the moment. How can I plead with innocence? This is my hour of betrayal, the guilt I hold like sand in my hands, it falls through my fingers and catches the wind, and I have no anger, just the man.

I face the journey home, each step brings me closer to reality, and each step brings me to warmth I do not deserve. The security of my mother's warmth. The son she gave life with pain of birth.

My journey home can never be too long, each step brings my fear closer, is this the time you asked me to follow my road with a dream of love? How can I ask for truth or happiness? This has no meaning to me.

Do not run from my honour I did as I was asked. It cannot be reached by the prayers of my lonely moments. If I cannot stand in all this pity, I do not deserve any re-assurance of love. I came to you in my hope. I came to you because this is my home. I have no understanding of my action. If I ask you to forgive me, stand before me while I kneel and I cry, watch the suffering, see my open feelings, do not see with my eyes, just let me return to my child. I ask for your arms, please protect me from my evil, and please protect me from my nightmares. When I awake, reach me with the warmth of your touch on my face. Let me look into your eyes and see the beauty of my surroundings. My journey home is complete. I have left the battlefield my war is finally over.

Andrew C Brown

Plate

I sit and stare at his meal
Its delicacies please the eye but not the heart
This appetite will remain un-sated
by its meaninglessness
One by one morsels move around routinely
When I stare hard enough I see a face
Its smiles confidently hiding all its real ingredients
With charm and sheer bombastic front.
Unwrapped I see contempt and selfishness
Should I have expected any other?
Disappointment grows each day not in him
But myself for showing my treasured rainbow
So now I'm left to scrape this intimacy from the plate
Hiding shame beneath the unused napkin

Helen L. Barker

Touch

Do not touch me with your mind, feel me with your heart, develop me and cover my flesh with your richness.

I will allow you to explore my mind with your compassion. Search my inner soul; enjoy the moment with your tongue. Taste the love from my nectar; only the sweat from passion can quench our thirst.

If you never see my existence, acknowledge my presence. Remove my eye from your hand.

Your attempt to manipulate me is wasted on a hard ground; do not plant your seed here. Your harvest baits no crop.

Yield, remain on your knees. Bow your head. You have no development here.

Andrew C Brown

My Watery Environ

By day the noise obliterates all thoughts
A fuzzy static distracts logic
With no hope of re-tuning I file for time

By night when it's quiet
I have a new occupation
I sit and think and spin my thumbs in circles

He turns a tap
And a development of words spews out
Each woven from a 4am call

My watery environ
Cut loose from a straight jacket called Life
I love to swim with dolphins

Helen L. Barker

True Life with Love.

The reality of true emotion can take us to all sorts of places we don't want to go.

I remember witnessing an accident that will stay with me for the rest of my life. I was in the Middle East, driving down a busy highway; a young couple were driving when they crashed in front of my vehicle.

I stayed with the young couple that had been caught up in the accident, they were both seriously injured. They had been married six months she was Tunisian and very beautiful he was Palestinian a handsome man, I stayed with them she died while I held her hand, and the man later died in hospital. I met both their families; the concept of religion had no place with us, just the sadness of lost children.

I will never forget how the women held my hand, and how her life switched to a peaceful everlasting sleep. The new life parted in tragic circumstances that could have been avoided. Her true Love followed her sleep twelve hours later.

Andrew C Brown

Loch Dreams

Day has followed night after day and still he sits
In his dreams they have talked as friends and lovers
He's cast words across books with her inspiration
Without her, his page is blank
He looks across the loch and still he waits
There is a fine mist lightly coating the water's surface
A setting sun highlights the edge of smoky waters
And a pinky hue warms the damp air
Through this ethereal setting faint beats echo
His imagination or his heart?
Neither the gravel nor the midges can distract
This single determination to meet destiny
Indefinable notes mingle in metered melody
Augmented by the stillness of the loch
A lilting hum graduates to more discernable
Celestial chants: a choir from a solo voice
Standing to scrutinize the expanse
Primed now but still he waits
As a sweet smell or is it taste that lingers
Furthering his need for her
Then through volatilising fumes
An outstretched hand is offered
His senses captivated by this goddess
Inside and out: an enchanting definition
He knows his waiting is over
Her final piece, his realisation, his dream unlocked
His open book of words remains on the bank,
A perfect epitaph as he wades out to meet his muse

Helen L. Barker

Walking by your Side

I will remember you in time; my mind will visit a distant memory and recall a smile or a little sadness.

If I remain in the heart I am a pilgrim who walks at your side to offer you guidance and direction in a life of fear and turmoil.

Do not ask of me a cure but ask of me the strength you deserve to continue your journey, I will oblige and hold out my arm for your support!!

Walk with me; let me guide you through all the hurdles of life. I will remain here at your side. Never again will you walk in darkness!

Andrew C Brown

The Palm Reader

On my palm sits a Rubik's puzzle
He uncurls my fingers to ponder
Gazing into smoky blue
I'm led through the maze.
At the centre: a box of pieces
I peer in but cannot see
Encouraged to use my inheritance
Grand parental eyes in today's world
This is their greatest legacy to me

With a previous generation's insight
Step by step I climb helical links
I use this to my own end
I can inhale their emotions
And breathe out their thoughts
A beneficiary of their experience and
With Kekulé's inspiration
I see the solution, I have the answer
Resolution by a dreamy reasoning

Helen L. Barker

Walls

Six by four the walls close in: the small window throws the light into the corner and feeds a shadowed room made of brick and bar.

One door in and one door out slammed shut in metal three inches thick. I have only hope filled with despair. The isolation smells like the loneliness of a cemetery. Each reason we ask why but who knows the regrettable feelings that honour the moment?

I feel the coldness of the room and touch the brick with soft fingertip. Ten feet thick with stone of time the walls hold the line between freedom and capture.

In the walls the world closes in and time stands still, and can we survive in this isolation?

Time to escape, just close your eyes, I can see a palm tree and a sailing boat on a blue sea. Maybe this is not so bad. Tomorrow I visit the mountains.

Andrew C Brown.

Daisy Chains

sun shines brightly on strawberry-cheeked innocence
fine white petals and sweet corn yellow florets
woven tenderly into priceless chains

high on the step sits the priestess
dark eyes stare bitterly out thro' sallow complexion
long since fallen into the hollowness of the bowl
filling it with more tears than peas
hating her existence and everyone that spins around her

her little satellite darts through the long grass
rosebud hands offering up to the altar
a sweet token of purity, freshness and love.

mechanically wincing a smile and a nod of acceptance
as the gift is laid carefully beside the emotionless vessel, used and empty.
Degraded by menial domesticity, her task is done.
Anger and resentment force her stride into the house leaving
the daisy chains strewn over the compost heap

Helen L Barker

We Came to Visit

We stand and watch with disbelieving eyes, what have they done?
We stand with the sweet grass around our feet we look down at the world with sadness.
The black surrounds the small pockets of bright colours that survive in unique possibilities. Each moment of hope, shining from the darkness.
We looked for the humanity among the squalid ness. Seeking out moments of life that can spread through the disgust.
The smell lingers above the sanctity of bright red, blue and yellow; all around stands discrimination, hatred and the horrific multiplex of man against man.

Each passing moment of time offers disease, unkindness and unspeakable cruelty, the good battles each segment of evil, the colour remains in the sea of blackness. In history they repeat the unbreakable cycle. Learning has no meaning; they continue to build, laying each block on a foundation of contaminated realism.

We turn away and walk on the sweet green grass, each step we contemplate the previous vision. How can they do such despicable cruel molestation? Each step brings more silence from the young ones, a tear fall from the cheek of innocence. One question burns in each mind.

We stop and remember; in the circle of expression the young asked only one question. That place, what do they call that place of sadness?

We can only be truthful in our answer. Earth!

Andrew C Brown

Angels

I did not get the time to say goodbye
When I left the room I heard them cry
The angel came to my bed, he rested his hand on my head
All the pain lifted and floated away
I knew I had to leave I couldn't stay
I wish I could have said goodbye, but all the tears
washed my soul, now I go to see the good, but do not forget
I will protect you where ever you go.

Now angelic, I take you by the hand
gently lead you into hills of sand
a warm carpet's toes one by one
shielding your soul from a burning sun
naked and vulnerable I offer meagre existence
to a presence that overwhelms all senses
unnerved: no surprise or fear of pain
a lifetime's heaviness was lifted in the rain
to melt into the familiarity of the guide
utterly loved and protected at your side

Andrew C Brown

Helen L Barker

Sense on Sense

Do not forsake me or leave my side
I only ask for a true emotion
My Love for you will feed from the passion you give
It takes my soul with tender hand and leads me to a sanctuary
I feel for you in my torment and you lead me to a place
This is my love and only love. I offer without condition.

next to you is not enough
I feel your breath on my skin
I hold your gaze with soft brown eyes
I cherish words of love in tiny goblets
and drink sweet wine of you
entwined your nearness soaks my senses
in a heady perfume of you my love
tonight I drown a happy man

Andrew C Brown

Helen L Barker